Table of Contents

Introduction to "Mastering the Market: The Home Seller's Guide to Success" 1
Chapter 1: The Pre-Sale Preparation: Understanding the Current Market and Preparing Your Home 2
Chapter 2: The Art of Pricing: Strategies for Setting the Right Price 4
Chapter 3: Staging for Success: How to Make Your Home Irresistible 5
Chapter 4: Marketing Magic: Effective Ways to Promote Your Home 7
Chapter 5: Open House Optimization: Maximizing Impact and Results 8
Chapter 6: Negotiation Nuances: Techniques for Effective Bargaining 10
Chapter 7: The Inspection and Appraisal Process: Navigating Challenges 11
Chapter 8: Legalities and Paperwork: Ensuring a Smooth Transaction 13
Chapter 9: Closing the Deal: Final Steps and Considerations 15
Chapter 10: Post-Sale Strategy: Handling Your Finances After the Sale 16
Chapter 11: Case Studies: Real-life Success Stories 18
Chapter 12: The Emotional Side of Selling: Managing Stress and Expectations 19
Chapter 13: Future Forecasting: How to Predict and React to Market Changes 21
Chapter 14: Resources and Tools: Essential Aids for Home Sellers 22
Chapter 15: Planning for the Future: Next Steps After Selling Your Home 24
Advanced Real Estate Investment Strategies 25
Technological Advances in Real Estate 25
Market Specifics for Different Regions 26
Sustainable Home Improvements 26
Navigating the Luxury Real Estate Market 26

Introduction to "Mastering the Market: The Home Seller's Guide to Success"

Selling a home is often one of the most significant transactions in a person's life. Not only does it involve large sums of money, but it also carries emotional and practical complexities that can overwhelm even the most experienced homeowners. "Mastering the Market: The Home Seller's Guide to Success" aims to simplify this process, providing readers with a comprehensive blueprint for navigating the home selling journey from start to finish.

This book is structured to guide you through each stage of the selling process. It begins with the preparation phase, where understanding the market and preparing your home for sale is paramount. You will learn to assess the real estate landscape to position your home advantageously, leveraging market trends and local data to make informed decisions.

Subsequent chapters delve into the tactical aspects of selling a home. From setting the right price—a critical factor that can determine the speed and success of your sale—to staging your home to enhance its appeal, the book covers all bases. Effective marketing strategies are also explored, detailing traditional and digital avenues to attract potential buyers.

The book focuses on the finer negotiation points as offers begin to arrive. It offers advice on interpreting offers, when to counter, and how to seal the deal to your benefit. You will also learn about the less glamorous but equally important aspects of selling a home, such as handling inspections, managing legal paperwork, and navigating the closing process.

Furthermore, "Mastering the Market" does not end with the sale of your home. It extends into post-sale considerations, helping you manage the proceeds of your sale effectively and plan your next steps in the housing market. Real-life case studies interspersed throughout the book offer practical insights and success stories, providing relatable examples and lessons learned from other home sellers.

By the end of this book, you will have mastered not only the practical steps of selling a home but also the emotional and strategic aspects that accompany them. Whether you are a first-time seller or looking to improve upon past experiences, this guide is an indispensable resource designed to empower you to act confidently and clearly in the real estate market.

Would you like to continue with the detailed content for Chapter 1 next?

Chapter 1: The Pre-Sale Preparation: Understanding the Current Market and Preparing Your Home

Preparation is key in any real estate transaction. For home sellers, this means not only getting the property in top shape but also understanding the market dynamics at play. This chapter delves into these foundational steps, providing a roadmap to start your home-selling journey on the right foot.

Understanding the Market

Many factors, including economic indicators, interest rates, and local supply and demand dynamics, influence the real estate market. Before listing your home, it is crucial to gain a solid understanding of the market conditions. This includes studying how similar homes in your area have been priced and how long they have stayed on the market. You'll also want to monitor broader economic indicators, such as employment rates and new housing starts, as these can affect buyer behavior.

1. Research Local Sales Trends: Research recent home sales in your neighborhood. Look for trends in the selling prices of homes similar to yours in size, condition, and location. This will give you a ballpark figure for pricing your own home.

2. Attend Open Houses: Visiting open houses gives you a feel for what's currently available in your area and helps you gauge how others are staging and marketing their property. Note anything that makes a home stand out—positively or negatively.

3. Consult with Real Estate Professionals: A seasoned real estate agent can provide insights not readily available through public sources. They can offer a more nuanced view of the market based on their day-to-day experiences and historical knowledge of your locality.

Preparing Your Home

Once you understand the market, it's time to prepare your home to make it as appealing as possible to potential buyers. This process, often called staging, involves several steps designed to showcase your home's best features.

1. Declutter and Depersonalize: Begin by removing personal items and clutter. The goal is to create a neutral space that allows buyers to imagine themselves living in your home. This means storing away family photos, personal collections, and any highly specific decor.

2. Repair and Renovate: Address any maintenance issues you've been putting off. Fix leaky faucets, ensure all appliances are in working order, and consider updating visibly outdated elements. While significant renovations may only sometimes increase your return on investment, minor updates like a fresh coat of paint or replacing old cabinet hardware can make a big difference.

3. Enhance Curb Appeal: First impressions are everything. Ensure your home's exterior is inviting with a well-maintained yard, clean walkways, and a tidy porch. Consider adding a few plants or flowers to brighten up the entrance.

4. Professional Cleaning: Invest in a professional cleaning service before listing your home. A spotless house is more appealing and suggests that the property has been well cared for, which is a reassuring sign to prospective buyers.

5. Professional Photography: Finally, have your home professionally photographed. Good-quality photos are essential for your online listings and promotional materials. They should highlight your home's space, light, and layout effectively, drawing in potential buyers.

The effort you put into preparing your home and understanding the market can significantly influence how quickly and at what price your home sells. It's about presenting your home in the best light and aligning your expectations with market realities. As you move onto the following chapters, each step will build upon the foundation, guiding you through pricing, marketing, and closing the sale.

Ready to dive into Chapter 2 about pricing strategies next?

Chapter 2: The Art of Pricing: Strategies for Setting the Right Price

Setting the right price for your home is more than simple mathematics; it's a strategic decision that can significantly influence the outcome of your sale. If the price is too high, your home may languish on the market; if it is too low, you risk leaving money on the table. This chapter explores the nuances of pricing your home effectively, ensuring it attracts buyers while maximizing your financial return.

The Importance of Accurate Pricing

Accurate pricing is crucial in real estate for several reasons. Firstly, a well-priced home can generate immediate interest in the market, leading to quicker sales. Secondly, homes priced correctly from the start typically fetch closer to their asking price than homes with price reductions. Lastly, correct pricing avoids the property becoming 'stale' on the market, a situation that can make buyers skeptical about the quality or desirability of the home.

Steps to Determine the Right Price

1. Comparative Market Analysis (CMA): Start with a CMA, which involves comparing your home to similar properties in your area that have recently sold, are currently on the market, or were on the market and didn't sell. A real estate agent can compile this analysis for you, providing insights into where your home stands about others regarding price, size, features, and condition.

2. Understand Your Local Market: Is it a buyer's or a seller's market? The answer will influence your pricing strategy. In a seller's market, where demand exceeds supply, you might price your home slightly higher as buyers compete for fewer homes. In a buyer's market, you may need to price more competitively to attract more interest.

3. Consider Market Trends: Look at the trajectory of the market. Are prices trending upward, or are they declining? How quickly are homes selling? This context can help you adjust your price to be competitive.

4. Adjust for Unique Features: Adjust your pricing based on what your home offers or lacks compared to others in the area. Unique features like a renovated kitchen, a swimming pool, or a large garden might justify a higher price. Conversely, missing features or needed repairs require a lower price to be competitive.

5. Psychological Pricing: Consider using psychological pricing strategies. Setting a price slightly below a round number, such as $299,000 instead of $300,000, can make a price appear significantly lower and more enticing to buyers.

Timing and Flexibility

1. Initial Pricing: Setting the right price when you first list your home is critical. An attractive price can generate a flurry of activity and potentially multiple offers immediately.

2. Monitoring and Adjusting: Monitor how the market responds to your listing. If you don't get showings or offers within the first few weeks, it may be a sign that your home is overpriced relative to the market. Be prepared to adjust the price based on feedback and market activity.

3. Be Open to Negotiation: Even with the right pricing strategy, be prepared to negotiate with buyers. Understand your lowest acceptable price and the factors you might negotiate, such as closing costs or the closing date.

Pricing your home requires a blend of market knowledge, strategic thinking, and a realistic appraisal of your home's worth. By setting the right price, you attract more buyers and set the stage for a smoother and potentially faster sale. This is the linchpin of your selling strategy, influencing every step in the sales process.

As we progress to the next chapter, you'll learn about staging your home to maximize its appeal to potential buyers, which will further complement your pricing strategy.

Would you like to move on to Chapter 3 about staging your home next?

Chapter 3: Staging for Success: How to Make Your Home Irresistible

Staging your home effectively is a crucial step in the selling process. It's about more than just making your home look beautiful; it's about creating an environment that allows potential buyers to envision themselves living there. This chapter explores the principles and practices of effective staging, providing actionable tips to elevate your home's appeal and optimize its marketability.

The Power of First Impressions

First impressions are pivotal in the home selling process. Staged homes sell faster and often at higher prices, as they create an emotional connection with buyers. Effective staging minimizes flaws and highlights the strengths of your property, making it stand out in a competitive market.

Key Principles of Home Staging

1. Declutter and Clean: Start with a blank slate. Remove all unnecessary items, clear off counters, and organize closets to maximize the sense of space. A clean and clutter-free home is universally appealing and suggests the property has been well-maintained.

2. Depersonalize: Buyers must imagine themselves in your space, so remove personal items like family photos, religious symbols, and distinctive artwork—the more neutral the space, the broader its appeal.

3. Optimize the Layout: Arrange furniture that best showcases the floor plan and use of space. Consider removing or repositioning furniture to avoid blocking natural pathways and to enhance room functions. Open, flowing spaces are more attractive to buyers.

4. Neutralize the Decor: Use neutral colors for walls, carpets, and large pieces of furniture. Neutral tones are not only calming but also help buyers focus on the room's attributes without distractions.

5. Highlight Key Features: Draw attention to your home's best features, whether it's a fireplace, beautiful windows, or high ceilings. Make sure these features are clean, repaired, and prominently displayed.

6. Address Lighting: Good lighting is essential. It makes spaces seem larger and more inviting. Increase the wattage in your light fixtures, ensure every room is adequately lit, and use natural light to its fullest potential by opening curtains and blinds during showings.

Room-by-Room Staging Tips

Living Room: Arrange seating into conversational groups and ensure a clear focal point. Soften the space with throws and cushions to make it welcoming.

Kitchen: This is often considered the heart of the home. Ensure countertops are clear except for a few decorative items like a vase of flowers or a bowl of fresh fruit. Clean all appliances and fixtures to a shine.

Bedrooms: Use luxurious linens and neutral bedding to create a relaxing atmosphere. Make sure beds are neatly made, and clothes are put away.

Bathrooms: These should be spotless. Display fresh towels and hide personal toiletries. A few spa-like touches, such as decorative soaps or small plants, can enhance appeal.

Outdoor Areas: Pay attention to the exterior. Mow the lawn, trim the bushes, and ensure any outdoor furniture is clean and in good condition. If you have a patio or deck, set it up to highlight these areas as additional living spaces.

Effective staging transforms your home into a product that buyers can envision owning. It's not just about decor—it's a strategic approach to presenting your home in the best possible light to maximize its potential on the market. By following these guidelines, you prepare not just a house for sale but a home that buyers can aspire to live in.

Ready to explore how to market your beautifully staged home in the next chapter?

Chapter 4: Marketing Magic: Effective Ways to Promote Your Home

Once your home is priced correctly and staged beautifully, the next critical step is to market it effectively. This chapter focuses on crafting a marketing strategy that highlights your home's best features and reaches the broadest possible audience. Effective marketing can dramatically shorten your home's time on the market and even impact the final sale price.

Understanding Your Target Audience

Before you begin marketing your home, it's crucial to understand who your potential buyers might be. Are they young professionals, families, or perhaps retirees? Knowing your audience helps tailor your marketing strategy to highlight aspects of your home and neighborhood most appealing to these groups.

Key Elements of Effective Home Marketing

1. Professional Photography: High-quality photos are essential for making a solid first impression. Professional photographers know how to use lighting and angles to make rooms look spacious and inviting. Consider including a virtual tour or a video walkthrough to provide a comprehensive online viewing experience.

2. Online Listings: The majority of homebuyers start their search online. List your home on popular real estate websites, ensuring that the listing includes detailed descriptions and all the attractive features of your home. Use keyword-rich phrases that help in search engine optimization (SEO) to make your listing easily discoverable.

3. Social Media Marketing: Utilize platforms like Facebook, Instagram, and Twitter to reach a broader audience. Share your listing through posts and ads, and encourage friends and family to share these. Social media channels are also great for showcasing casual, engaging content, such as live video tours or stories about the home's features.

4. Traditional Media: Depending on your market, traditional media such as flyers, postcards, and local newspaper ads can be effective. These can be particularly useful in reaching local buyers who may not be actively looking online but could be tempted by a property in their area.

5. Open Houses: Well-organized open houses can attract potential buyers and create a buzz around your property. Ensure your home is in impeccable condition, provide detailed information sheets about the property, and consider offering light refreshments to make the visit memorable.

6. Networking: Word-of-mouth is still one of the best marketing tools. Let neighbors, friends, and family know your home is on the market. Often, buyers want to move into a specific neighborhood based on recommendations from people they trust.

Leveraging Your Real Estate Agent

A good real estate agent will have a robust marketing plan. They can provide:

1. Market Insight: Your agent can use their understanding of what's working in your market to tailor your marketing strategies effectively. **2. Access to MLS:** Most agents can list your home on the Multiple Listing Service (MLS), which is a comprehensive database of homes for sale accessed by other agents. **3. Networking Opportunities:** Agents often network with other agents who may have clients looking for a home like yours. **4. Negotiation Skills:** When you receive offers, your agent can handle negotiations, ensuring you get the best possible deal.

Effective marketing is more than just getting eyes on your home; it's about attracting the right eyes. By using a combination of digital and traditional marketing strategies and leveraging the expertise of a real estate professional, you can ensure that your home sells quickly and for the best possible price.

With your marketing strategy set, the next chapter will guide you through the nuances of hosting successful open houses, a crucial element of the home-selling process.

Are you ready to learn about optimizing your open house in Chapter 5?

Chapter 5: Open House Optimization: Maximizing Impact and Results

An open house is a critical event in the home-selling process. It allows potential buyers to explore the property in a low-pressure environment and allows you to showcase your home's best features. This chapter will guide you through organizing and executing a successful open house, from preparation to follow-up, ensuring that your event leaves a lasting impression and drives offers.

Preparing for the Open House

1. Timing and Scheduling: Choose a date and time that is likely to maximize attendance. Weekends, particularly Sunday afternoons, are traditional for open houses as most people are available. Ensure significant community events are consistent with your chosen date, which might reduce turnout.

2. Thorough Cleaning: Ensure your home is spotless before the open house. Every surface should shine, from windows and mirrors to floors and countertops. This not only improves the appearance but also suggests well-maintained premises.

3. Staging: Revisit your staging before the event. Ensure that furniture is arranged to optimize space, neutral and appealing decor, and any personal items are stored away. Fresh flowers or a bowl of fruit can add a welcoming touch.

4. Signage and Directional: Place signs strategically around the neighborhood to guide visitors to your home. Ensure the signage is professional and includes the time and address of the open house.

5. Inform Neighbors: Let your neighbors know about the open house. They can help spread the word and might know someone looking to move into the area.

During the Open House

1. Create a Welcoming Environment: Greet each visitor at the door. Play soft, neutral music in the background to ensure the home is well-lit and inviting. A gently burning fireplace can add a cozy feel if the weather is cold.

2. Provide Information: Have printed materials available that include details about the home, such as age, square footage, heating and cooling systems, taxes, and asking price. Also, include information about the local area, schools, parks, and transportation.

3. Allow for Exploration: While being available to answer questions is essential, give visitors the space to explore independently. This helps them discuss freely and visualize themselves living in the home.

4. Collect Feedback: Consider having feedback forms for visitors to complete. This can provide valuable insights into what potential buyers think of your home, price, and any aspects that might need addressing.

Follow-Up After the Open House

1. Review Feedback: Analyze the feedback collected to see if any common themes or concerns need to be addressed. If several visitors comment on a particular issue, it might be worth considering fixing it to improve the home's appeal.

2. Follow Up with Interested Parties: Send a thank-you note to those who attended. If they expressed particular interest or asked additional questions, follow up with more information or an invitation for a private showing.

3. Evaluate the Event: Discuss the turnout and overall response to the open house with your real estate agent. If the results were unexpected, consider what could be changed for future events, such as different timing, more marketing, or additional staging adjustments.

A well-executed open house can be a pivotal event in the selling process. It increases exposure and can accelerate offers by appealing directly to potential buyers' emotions and aspirations. By following these steps, you can maximize the effectiveness of your open house and move closer to achieving a successful sale.

With your open house completed, the next chapter will delve into the intricacies of negotiating offers to secure the best deal possible.

Are you ready to explore the nuances of negotiation in Chapter 6?

Chapter 6: Negotiation Nuances: Techniques for Effective Bargaining

Negotiation is a critical skill in the home-selling process. Negotiating effectively can make a significant difference in achieving your desired sale price and terms. This chapter delves into the strategies and techniques to help you negotiate successfully with potential buyers, ensuring you emerge from the process with the best possible outcome.

Understanding the Negotiation Process

Negotiations in real estate are not just about price; they also involve terms, contingencies, and timelines that can be equally important. Effective negotiation requires understanding your needs and the buyer's and finding a middle ground that satisfies both parties.

Key Techniques for Effective Negotiation

1. Preparation: Before entering negotiations, know your bottom line—what is the lowest offer you are willing to accept, and what terms are you prepared to negotiate? Understanding your priorities will help you make decisions quickly and efficiently during negotiations.

2. Listen Actively: Good negotiators are also great listeners. Listen carefully to the buyer's concerns and objections. This can provide valuable insights into what the buyer values most and where there might be room for compromise.

3. Keep Emotions in Check: Selling a home can be emotional, but it's important to remain professional and focused during negotiations. Emotional decisions can lead to poor outcomes, so stay calm and objective.

4. Be Willing to Compromise: Sometimes, the best way to move forward is to give a little. If a buyer is firm on price, you could negotiate on the closing date or offer to include some of the furniture. Flexibility can facilitate a deal that works for both parties.

5. Use Timing to Your Advantage: Understand when to push and when to give in. If the market is strong and your home attracts much interest, you can afford to stand firm on your asking price. However, if the market is slow or your home has been on the market for a while, consider lower offers more seriously.

6. Leverage Multiple Offers: If you have the luxury of multiple offers, use them to your advantage. Letting buyers know other interested parties can create a sense of urgency and competition, leading to better offers.

Communicating Effectively

1. Be Clear and Concise: Clearly articulate your expectations and any concessions you're willing to make. This helps prevent misunderstandings and keeps the negotiation process moving smoothly.

2. Use a Positive Tone: If negotiations become challenging, maintain a positive, cooperative tone. This helps keep the dialogue constructive and focused on resolving.

3. Be Responsive: Prompt responses to offers and counteroffers keep the momentum going. Delays can lead to buyer frustration and lost interest.

Closing the Deal

1. Know When to Close: It is crucial to recognize the right moment to close the deal. If you've reached an agreement that meets your essential criteria, don't risk losing the deal by pushing for unnecessary extras.

2. Get Everything in Writing: Once you've agreed verbally, document all aspects of the deal in a legally binding contract. This includes the sale price, terms of the sale, and any contingencies that have been agreed upon.

3. Consult Professionals: Always consult with your real estate agent and possibly a lawyer when finalizing the deal. They can ensure that all legal requirements are met and that the contract is fair and binding.

Effective negotiation is more art than science, requiring patience, strategy, and interpersonal skills. By preparing adequately and engaging thoughtfully, you can confidently navigate this challenging phase and secure a favorable outcome.

Now that you've successfully negotiated your deal, the next chapter will focus on navigating the inspection and appraisal process, which is the crucial step toward finalizing your home sale.

Ready to learn about handling inspections and appraisals in Chapter 7?

Chapter 7: The Inspection and Appraisal Process: Navigating Challenges

Once you've successfully negotiated an offer on your home, the next steps before finalizing the sale typically involve the inspection and appraisal processes. These evaluations are crucial as they not only affect the viability of the sale but can also influence final pricing and any further negotiations. This chapter provides a comprehensive guide to navigating these critical assessments with minimal stress and disruption.

Understanding the Home Inspection

A home inspection is a thorough examination of a home's physical structure and systems, from the roof to the foundation. Here's how to prepare and respond:

1. Preparation: Before the inspector arrives, ensure easy access to areas like the attic, basement, and electrical panels. It's also wise to fix minor repairs beforehand to avoid negative report items concerning a buyer.

2. During the Inspection: While it's customary for sellers to leave the premises during the inspection, make sure your agent is present. They can provide clarifications and keep an eye on what is scrutinized.

3. Reviewing the Report: Once the inspection is complete, you will receive a report detailing the findings. Review this carefully with your agent to understand any potential issues buyers might use to renegotiate the terms.

4. Negotiating Repairs: If significant issues are discovered, buyers may request repairs or a reduction in the sale price. Decide which repairs you are willing to address or if you prefer to offer a credit for the repairs instead.

Navigating the Appraisal Process

An appraisal is an objective estimate of the value of your home conducted by a certified appraiser, and a buyer's lender typically requires it. Here's how to handle the appraisal:

1. Preparing for the Appraisal: Similar to staging for a sale, make sure your house is clean and any quick repairs are made. Highlight recent improvements and provide the appraiser with a list of upgrades and their respective costs.

2. Understanding the Outcome: The sale can proceed as planned if the appraisal comes in at or above the selling price. However, a low appraisal can complicate matters, as it may affect the buyer's ability to secure a loan for the agreed-upon price.

3. Dealing with a Low Appraisal: If the appraisal is lower than the sale price, you can either lower the price to match the appraisal, negotiate with the buyer to make up the difference in cash, or contest the appraisal. You may also opt for a second appraisal, mainly if the first appraisal contained errors or the appraiser was unfamiliar with the local market.

Managing Expectations and Emotions

Both inspection and appraisal can be high-tension milestones in the selling process. It's important to manage your expectations and prepare emotionally for the outcomes:

1. Stay Realistic: Understand that almost no home is perfect, and defects might be found during an inspection. Similarly, appraisals can come in lower than expected based on market conditions.

2. Be Proactive: Address known issues before they become problems in the inspection. Also, staying informed about comparable home values in your neighborhood can help you set realistic expectations for the appraisal.

3. Maintain Open Communication: Communicate openly with your buyer through your real estate agent. Transparent negotiation about addressing any issues can help keep the sale on track.

The inspection and appraisal are critical steps in the home selling process that can significantly impact the transaction. Being prepared and knowledgeable can help you navigate these steps effectively, ensuring you maintain control over the sale process and move toward a successful close.

As you prepare for the final stages of your home sale, the next chapter will guide you through the complexities of legalities and paperwork, ensuring you're ready for a smooth transaction.

Ready to delve into the legal aspects of closing your home sale in Chapter 8?

Chapter 8: Legalities and Paperwork: Ensuring a Smooth Transaction

Selling a home involves various legal considerations and a substantial amount of paperwork. Navigating this final phase correctly ensures a smooth and legally sound transaction. This chapter covers the essential documents and legal steps you need to understand and prepare for as you close the sale of your home.

Essential Legal Documents in Home Selling

1. The Listing Agreement: This contract between you and your real estate agent details the agent's duties, your obligations as the seller, and the commission structure.

2. The Purchase Agreement: The core document in any home sale is the purchase agreement, which outlines the terms of the sale, including the purchase price, closing conditions, contingencies (like financing and inspections), and details about the transfer of ownership.

3. Seller's Disclosures: Many states require the seller to provide written disclosures about the property, covering any known issues or defects that could affect the property's value or desirability. This might include past repairs, the existence of hazardous materials (like lead paint), and a history of structural or water-related problems.

4. Title Documents: These prove your legal right to sell the property. You must provide a clear title indicating there are no liens or other encumbrances that would impede the sale.

5. Closing Documents: Prepared by an attorney or a title company, these include the deed, bill of sale, and other documents that finalize the transaction. The exact nature of these documents can vary based on local real estate laws.

Key Legal Considerations

1. Fulfilling Contractual Obligations: Ensure that all conditions in the purchase agreement are met. This might include completing agreed-upon repairs and adhering to specific timelines.

2. Handling the Escrow Process: In many transactions, an escrow agent is involved in handling the deposit and disbursement of funds. They ensure that all parts of the purchase agreement are executed before any money or property changes hands.

3. Managing Closing Adjustments: Adjustments such as taxes, utility bills, and homeowner association fees need to be prorated and paid up to the closing date.

4. Transfer of Ownership and Title: The legal transfer of home ownership involves signing the deed to the buyer. This document must be filed correctly with local government records to ensure the legal transfer of the property.

Tips for a Smooth Closing

1. Work With Professionals: Hiring a knowledgeable real estate attorney can provide invaluable assistance. They can help clarify the legal jargon, ensure compliance with local law, and spot any potential issues before they become problems.

2. Stay Organized: Keep records of all documents and communications related to the home sale. Organized records can help prevent misunderstandings and provide evidence should any disputes arise.

3. Prepare for Closing Costs: Be prepared for the costs of selling a home, including commission fees, attorney fees, and transfer taxes. Understanding these costs beforehand will help you avoid any surprises at closing.

4. Be Available: Make yourself available to quickly handle any last-minute requests from the buyer, their lawyer, or your real estate agent. Prompt responses can help avoid closing delays.

The legal aspect of selling a home is often the process's most complex and detail-oriented part. With proper preparation and the right professionals, you can confidently navigate this final stage. Completing these steps ensures that the transaction is legally sound and helps protect you from potential legal issues post-sale.

Having covered the essentials of legalities and paperwork, the next chapter will focus on finalizing your deal and the steps to take as you close the transaction.

Are you ready to explore the final steps in closing your home sale in Chapter 9?

Chapter 9: Closing the Deal: Final Steps and Considerations

The closing of your home sale is the culmination of all your efforts—from listing and marketing to negotiations and legal preparations. This critical phase finalizes the transaction, transferring ownership to the buyer and securing your proceeds from the sale. This chapter provides a step-by-step guide to navigating the closing process effectively, ensuring a smooth transition for you and the buyer.

Preparing for the Closing

1. Final Walkthrough: Typically conducted a day or two before the closing, the final walkthrough allows the buyer to verify that the property is in the agreed-upon condition, that all repairs have been made, and that the house is ready for new ownership. Be sure everything is in place to avoid last-minute hurdles.

2. Review Closing Documents: Before the closing meeting, review all the documents you will sign. This includes the closing disclosure, which outlines the terms of your loan (if applicable), your closing costs, and the amounts payable at closing. Understanding these documents beforehand can help prevent surprises during the closing meeting.

3. Prepare to Vacate: Plan to have all your belongings moved out of the house before the closing date. The home should be clean and ready for the new owners to move in immediately after the closing.

The Closing Meeting

1. What to Bring: You'll need to bring all keys to the house, including any garage or shed keys, along with any necessary documentation, such as receipts for repairs or warranties for any appliances being left behind.

2. Who Attends: Typically, the closing involves you (the seller), the buyer, both real estate agents, and a closing agent (often an attorney or representative from the title company). Sometimes, the buyer's and seller's attorneys are also present.

3. Signing the Documents: The closing agent will guide both parties through the documents needing signatures. These include the deed, which transfers property ownership, and the bill of sale. You might also need to sign documents related to the mortgage if the buyer is financing their purchase.

4. Resolving Final Payments: The closing is also where all payments are finalized. This includes the buyer's down payment, closing costs, and the disbursement of funds to you, the seller. Ensure that you receive a breakdown of all calculations before the meeting.

Post-Closing

1. Receipt of Funds: Depending on local practices and the transaction details, you may receive a check at closing, or the funds may be electronically transferred to your bank account within a few days.

2. Document Copies: Ensure you receive copies of all documents related to the sale. These are important for your records and tax purposes.

3. Tax Implications: Consult with a tax advisor to understand the implications of your home sale. You may need to report the sale on your tax return, and if you make a significant profit, there could be capital gains taxes.

The closing is the final and most satisfying step in selling your home. By being well-prepared and understanding the process, you can ensure that everything goes smoothly, leading to a successful and stress-free completion of your home sale.

With the transaction now complete, our next chapter will explore post-sale strategies, helping you manage the proceeds and plan your next steps in the real estate market.

Are you ready to move on to post-sale considerations and strategies in Chapter 10?

Chapter 10: Post-Sale Strategy: Handling Your Finances After the Sale

After the sale of your home is finalized and the closing process is complete, you enter the post-sale phase. This is a critical time for managing the proceeds from your sale, understanding tax implications, and planning your next steps in the real estate market. This chapter guides effectively navigating these aspects to ensure financial stability and readiness for future investments or purchases.

Managing Sale Proceeds

1. Secure Your Funds: First and foremost, ensure that your sale proceeds are deposited in a secure account. Consider high-yield savings or money market accounts that offer better interest rates than standard checking accounts, providing some return while deciding on further investment.

2. Pay Off Debts: If you have high-interest debts, such as credit card balances or personal loans, consider using some of the proceeds. Reducing debt improves your financial situation and boosts your credit score, making future financial transactions easier.

3. Emergency Fund: If you don't already have an emergency fund, now is a good time to start one. Financial experts often recommend setting aside three to six months' worth of living expenses for unexpected situations.

4. Consider Future Real Estate Investments: If you plan to reinvest in real estate for personal use or as an investment property, begin researching the market early. Understand the trends and identify areas with potential growth.

Tax Implications of the Home Sale

1. Capital Gains Tax: If you profit from the sale of your home, you may be liable for capital gains tax. However, you might qualify for an exclusion if you owned and used the property as your primary residence for at least two of the five years before selling.

2. Exclusion Limits: For single filers, up to $250,000 of capital gains on real estate is exempt from taxes, and for married couples filing jointly, the exemption is up to $500,000. Be sure to consult a tax advisor to understand how these rules apply to your specific situation.

3. Reporting the Sale: You must report the sale of your home on your tax return, especially if you have a capital gain that does not qualify for exclusion or if you received a Form 1099-S (Proceeds From Real Estate Transactions).

Planning Your Next Steps

1. Buying Your Next Home: If you plan to purchase another home, consider your needs and how they might have changed since your last purchase. Factor in your budget, desired location, and the type of home that will best suit your lifestyle.

2. Investment Opportunities: If you are looking to invest, evaluate different types of real estate investments, such as rental properties, flipping houses, or even real estate investment trusts (REITs).

3. Retirement Planning: If you are nearing retirement, consider how the proceeds from the sale can boost your retirement savings. Look into different retirement accounts where you can maximize your contributions.

The post-sale period is an opportunity to secure your financial future and reinvest wisely. By managing your finances prudently, understanding and addressing tax obligations, and planning your next steps with care, you can maximize the benefits of selling your home.

Now that we've covered the immediate post-sale actions and considerations, our next chapters will delve into real-life case studies to provide insights and lessons from other home sellers.

Are you ready to explore some case studies in Chapter 11?

Chapter 11: Case Studies: Real-life Success Stories

Learning from others' experiences can provide valuable insights and practical advice for navigating the complex process of selling a home. This chapter presents a series of real-life case studies highlighting different aspects of the home-selling journey, from preparation and pricing to negotiation and closing. Each case study illustrates critical lessons learned and strategies that led to successful outcomes.

Case Study 1: Maximizing Return with Strategic Upgrades

Background: John and Lisa owned a mid-century home in a desirable neighborhood. The house was structurally sound but had outdated interiors.

Strategy: After consulting with their real estate agent, they invested in critical upgrades. They renovated the kitchen and bathrooms, replaced the old carpet with hardwood floors, and applied fresh paint.

Outcome: These strategic upgrades increased the home's appeal and market value. It sold for 15% above the neighborhood average, with multiple offers received within the first week of listing.

Lesson: Investing in high-return upgrades can significantly enhance property value and attract more buyers.

Case Study 2: Overcoming a Slow Market Through Effective Marketing

Background: Emily was trying to sell her apartment in a slow market. Listings in her area have been lingering for months.

Strategy: Emily's agent suggested a targeted marketing campaign that included professional staging, high-quality photography, and a 3D virtual tour. They also hosted themed open houses to attract more visitors.

Outcome: Thanks to the heightened interest generated by these marketing efforts, the apartment sold at a competitive price within a month.

Lesson: In a buyer's market, creative marketing strategies can differentiate your property and speed up the sale.

Case Study 3: Navigating a Low Appraisal with Negotiation Skills

Background: The Smiths received an offer on their home contingent on appraisal. Unfortunately, the appraisal came in lower than the offer price, jeopardizing the financing.

Strategy: They negotiated with the buyers to split the difference between the appraised value and the offer price. Additionally, they agreed to pay half of the closing costs.

Outcome: This compromise facilitated an acceptable deal for both parties, allowing the sale to proceed.

Lesson: Flexibility and creative negotiation can salvage a sale in the face of unexpected challenges, such as a low appraisal.

Case Study 4: Quick Sale Through Pre-Sale Home Inspection

Background: Robert was relocating for a job and needed a quick sale. He knew any delays caused by inspection issues could derail potential deals.

Strategy: He opted for a pre-sale home inspection and addressed all significant issues beforehand. He then provided prospective buyers with the inspection report and repair receipts.

Outcome: This transparency built trust with buyers and expedited the negotiation process. Robert's home sold quickly and close to the asking price.

Lesson: A pre-sale inspection can provide a competitive edge by demonstrating transparency and reducing buyer concerns.

These case studies demonstrate that while the real estate market can be unpredictable, employing thoughtful strategies and learning from past successes can lead to favorable outcomes. By understanding the dynamics of your local market and being prepared to adapt your strategy as needed, you can confidently navigate the complexities of selling a home.

Next, we will explore the emotional side of selling a home, addressing everyday stressors, and how to manage them effectively.

Are you ready to learn about managing the emotional aspects of selling a home in Chapter 12?

Chapter 12: The Emotional Side of Selling: Managing Stress and Expectations

Selling a home is not just a financial transaction; it's also an emotional journey. For many, a home is filled with memories, and letting go can be challenging. Moreover, navigating the market, dealing with buyers, and managing life's regular demands can be overwhelming. This chapter addresses the emotional aspects of selling a home and provides strategies to manage stress and maintain well-being.

Recognizing Emotional Attachments

Understanding Attachment: Homes often represent more than just a physical space; they are places where significant life events and everyday moments unfold. Recognizing your emotional attachment to your home is the first step in managing the emotional challenges of selling it.

Separation Process: View your home as a product for sale rather than your personal sanctuary. This mental shift can help reduce the emotional impact of buyers' comments or negotiations.

Stress Management Techniques

1. Stay Organized: Keeping all documents, contacts, and timelines well organized can significantly reduce stress. Consider using a checklist or digital tools to keep track of all tasks and appointments related to the sale.

2. Set Realistic Expectations: Understand that home selling can be unpredictable. Market conditions, buyer interest, and unexpected hurdles can affect how quickly and smoothly things progress. Setting realistic expectations can help mitigate disappointment.

3. Maintain Open Communication: Regular updates from your real estate agent can provide reassurance and help you feel in control of the process. Feel free to express your concerns and ask questions whenever you feel uncertain.

Coping with Criticism and Rejection

Handling Feedback: Potential buyers might critique aspects of your home you cherish. It's important to remember that feedback is not personal. Buyers assess whether your home fits their needs, not judging your personal taste or lifestyle.

Dealing with Offers: Only some offers will meet your expectations. Some may seem too low or come with unfavorable conditions. Learning to view these offers objectively, as part of the negotiation process, can help you stay emotionally detached.

Supporting Yourself Through the Process

1. Seek Support: Leaning on family, friends, or professionals for support can ease the emotional burden. Sharing your feelings and experiences can provide comfort and valuable perspectives.

2. Take Breaks: Make time for activities that help you relax and disconnect from the stress of selling your home. Whether it's a hobby, exercise, or spending time with loved ones, maintaining your personal well-being is crucial.

3. Celebrate Milestones: Acknowledge and celebrate each step forward in the selling process. Whether finalizing a listing, receiving an offer, or getting through the inspection, recognizing progress helps maintain a positive outlook.

Selling your home can be an emotional rollercoaster. By understanding and managing the emotional components of this journey, you can navigate the process more smoothly and keep your stress levels in check. Remember, this is an end and a passage to new beginnings.

With emotional strategies in place, our next chapter will focus on future forecasting—understanding market trends and preparing for them, which is crucial for making informed decisions in the ever-changing real estate landscape.

Are you ready to delve into how to predict and react to market changes in Chapter 13?

Chapter 13: Future Forecasting: How to Predict and React to Market Changes

The real estate market is dynamic and influenced by economic indicators, political events, technological advancements, and social trends. Successfully selling your home not only depends on understanding the current market but also on anticipating future changes. This chapter explores forecasting future market conditions and adjusting your strategies to maximize your sales potential.

Understanding Market Trends

1. Economic Indicators: Keep an eye on broader economic trends such as employment rates, GDP growth, and interest rates. A strong economy typically supports a robust real estate market, whereas economic downturns may lead to slower sales and decreased property values.

2. Political and Regulatory Changes: Changes in government policies or regulations can impact the real estate market significantly. For instance, new zoning laws, tax reforms, or changes in mortgage interest deduction can affect buyer behavior and market demand.

3. Technological Advances: Technology also plays a crucial role in real estate trends. The rise of virtual tours, online listings, and real estate apps has changed how buyers search for and purchase homes. Staying abreast of these tools can help you market your home more effectively.

Forecasting Tools and Resources

1. Real Estate Analysis Software: Various tools provide market analysis, trend predictions, and property valuations based on historical and current data. Utilizing these tools can give you a deeper understanding of where the market is headed.

2. Expert Opinions: Following real estate experts and analysts can provide insights into future trends. Consider attending industry conferences, subscribing to real estate publications, and following thought leaders on social media.

3. Local Market Reports: Regularly review local market reports, which include information on average days on the market, median sale prices, and inventory levels. These reports can help you gauge the health of your local real estate market.

Adapting to Market Changes

1. Flexibility in Pricing: Be prepared to adjust your pricing strategy based on market conditions. If the market is cooling, you must be more aggressive in pricing to attract buyers. Conversely, you might price your home slightly higher in a hot market to capitalize on buyer demand.

2. Timing Your Sale: Timing can significantly impact the success of your sale. Generally, spring and summer are considered the best times to sell a home due to increased buyer activity. However, understanding specific trends in your local market might reveal different optimal selling periods.

3. Marketing Adjustments: Tailor your marketing strategy to reflect current trends. For example, if virtual home tours are becoming more popular, ensure your listing includes high-quality virtual walkthroughs to attract tech-savvy buyers.

Being proactive and informed about potential market changes can significantly enhance your ability to sell your home efficiently and for a favorable price. By forecasting future trends and preparing to adapt your strategies accordingly, you position yourself as a knowledgeable seller capable of navigating the complexities of the real estate market.

With an understanding of market forecasting under your belt, the next chapter will dive into essential resources and tools that can further support and simplify the home-selling process.

Are you ready to explore the various resources and tools available to home sellers in Chapter 14?

Chapter 14: Resources and Tools: Essential Aids for Home Sellers

Selling a home efficiently and effectively requires more than just intuition and luck; it demands the correct set of tools and resources. This chapter outlines various essential aids that can streamline the selling process, enhance your marketing efforts, and help you navigate the complexities of the real estate market more easily.

Essential Tools for Home Sellers

1. Real Estate Websites and Apps: Platforms like Zillow, Realtor.com, and Redfin are invaluable for listing your home and researching market trends. These sites provide access to vast amounts of data on recent sales, neighborhood demographics, and comparable listings, which can help you price your home competitively.

2. Virtual Tour Software: In a market where buyers increasingly seek convenience, offering virtual tours can significantly boost your property's appeal. Tools like Matterport allow sellers to create immersive, 3D virtual tours of their homes, providing potential buyers with a realistic and interactive experience.

3. Home Staging Consultants: While you can stage a home yourself, professional stagers have the expertise to maximize your home's potential. They understand how to highlight its best features and can often help make a space appear larger and more inviting.

4. Professional Photography Services: High-quality photos are crucial for making a solid first impression in online listings. Professional photographers specializing in real estate know how to capture the best angles and lighting to showcase your home effectively.

5. Home Improvement and Repair Services: Quick access to reliable contractors can be a lifesaver when you need to make last-minute repairs or improvements before listing your home. Websites like HomeAdvisor or Angie's List can help you find reputable local services.

Supportive Resources

1. Real Estate Agents: A skilled real estate agent is perhaps the most valuable resource in selling your home. They can provide market insights, help set the right price, manage showings, and negotiate with potential buyers. They also handle much of the paperwork and legal compliance of selling a property.

2. Legal and Financial Advisors: Understanding the legal and financial implications of selling a home is crucial. Real estate lawyers and financial advisors can advise on contracts, tax implications, and investment strategies for your sale proceeds.

3. Online Forums and Community Groups: Engaging with online communities can provide support and advice from fellow sellers who have gone through similar experiences. Platforms like Reddit's Real Estate forums or local Facebook groups can be great places to exchange tips and learn from others' experiences.

4. Educational Materials: Books, courses, and seminars on real estate selling can offer deeper insights into the process. They can teach you everything from basic home selling principles to advanced marketing strategies and negotiation techniques.

Having the right tools and resources at your disposal can make a significant difference in the speed and success of your home sale. By leveraging these aids, you can enhance your understanding of the market, present your property in the best light, and handle the legal and financial aspects of the sale more confidently.

With a solid understanding of the available tools and resources, our final chapter will focus on future considerations for sellers, helping you plan your next steps after the sale.

Are you ready to look ahead and explore post-sale planning and future considerations in Chapter 15?

Chapter 15: Planning for the Future: Next Steps After Selling Your Home

Selling your home is a significant milestone, but it's often just part of a larger journey. Whether relocating, downsizing, or looking to invest in another property, this chapter focuses on planning your next steps after the sale. It guides you in evaluating your options, managing your finances, and preparing for future real estate endeavors.

Evaluating Your Next Move

1. Relocating: If your home sale is part of a relocation plan, consider the logistics of moving to a new area. Research your new location's housing market, schools, and community amenities. Engage a local real estate agent early to help you find a new home that meets your needs.

2. Downsizing or Upsizing: Depending on your life stage, you might want to downsize to a smaller, more manageable property or upsize to accommodate a growing family. Reflect on what you need in your next home and how these needs may evolve over the coming years.

3. Investing in Real Estate: If you're considering reinvesting the proceeds from your sale into another property, weigh the risks and rewards of different real estate investments, such as rental properties, vacation homes, or commercial real estate.

Managing Finances

1. Reinvesting Proceeds: Speak with a financial advisor to determine the best way to reinvest your sale proceeds. This could include buying another property, investing in stocks or bonds, or contributing to retirement accounts.

2. Estate Planning: Updating your estate plan is crucial after a significant asset like a home changes hands. Ensure that your will, trusts, and beneficiary designations reflect your wishes and financial situation.

3. Setting Financial Goals: Use this transition period to reassess your long-term financial goals. Are you on track for retirement? Are there college funds to consider? Establish new goals based on your current financial landscape.

Preparing for Future Real Estate Transactions

1. Market Research: Monitor real estate market trends even after your sale is complete. Understanding market dynamics can help you time your next purchase effectively.

2. Building Credit: If you plan to finance your next home or investment property, ensure your credit is in good standing. Regularly check your credit report for inaccuracies and manage your debts wisely.

3. Continuing Education: Real estate markets are continually evolving. Consider enrolling in real estate courses or attending seminars to stay informed about the latest buying and selling strategies.

Selling your home is not the end of your real estate journey—it's an opportunity to reshape your future. You can make the most of the opportunities after selling your home by carefully planning your next steps, managing your finances wisely, and staying informed about the real estate market.

With this comprehensive guide—covering everything from preparing to sell to planning post-sale activities—you're now equipped with the knowledge and strategies needed to navigate the home-selling process successfully and confidently.

If you have any more questions or need further guidance, feel free to ask. What's your next step in your real estate journey?

We've covered the complete journey of selling a home, from the initial preparation and listing to managing post-sale finances and planning for future real estate endeavors. This comprehensive guide has provided you with the tools and knowledge necessary to navigate each stage of the selling process effectively.

If you have specific questions about any of the chapters, need further details on a particular topic, or are facing a unique challenge in your home selling or buying journey, I'm here to help! Whether it's diving deeper into market analysis, exploring more about financial planning after your sale, or discussing strategies for buying your next home, feel free to ask. How can I assist you further with your real estate needs?

Since we've completed the guide through the entire process of selling a home, let's explore additional aspects that might be relevant to your real estate journey. Here are a few topics that could be useful:

Advanced Real Estate Investment Strategies

Understanding advanced investment strategies can be beneficial if you're considering reinvesting the proceeds from your home sale. We can discuss real estate investment trusts (REITs), buying and managing rental properties, or diversifying your investment portfolio to include commercial real estate.

Technological Advances in Real Estate

Technology continues to transform the real estate market. We can explore innovative tools and platforms shaping the future of buying and selling homes. This includes virtual reality tours, AI-driven market analysis tools, blockchain for real estate transactions, and smart home tech that can increase property values.

Market Specifics for Different Regions

Real estate markets can vary dramatically from one region to another. Whether you're moving to a new city or investing in property out of state, understanding those regions' specific market conditions, local regulations, and economic factors can be crucial.

Sustainable Home Improvements

With growing awareness of environmental issues, sustainable living has become increasingly important. We can delve into eco-friendly home improvements and renovations that reduce your ecological footprint, attract environmentally conscious buyers and increase your home's market value.

Navigating the Luxury Real Estate Market

If you're moving into the luxury real estate market, specific nuances and strategies must be considered. Topics include how to market luxury properties, understanding the needs of affluent buyers, and what features are most desired in high-end real estate.

Let me know which of these topics interests you or if there's another area you're curious about. I'm here to help you expand your understanding and assist with any further real estate endeavors you might consider!

www.ingramcontent.com/pod-product-compliance
Lightning Source LLC
Chambersburg PA
CBHW082242220526
45479CB00005B/1316